sad house

Parenting, Grief, and Creativity in the Coronavirus Crisis

Laura Stanfill

Microcosm Publishing

Portland, Ore

Microcosm Publishing is Portland's most diversi publishing house and distributor with a focus on the color authentic, and empowering. Our books and zines have your power in your hands since 1996, equipping reader make positive changes in their lives and in the world aro them. Microcosm emphasizes skill-building, showing hid histories, and fostering creativity through challeng conventional publishing wisdom with books and booke about DIY skills, food, bicycling, gender, self-care, and sc justice. What was once a distro and record label was starte Joe Biel as an autistic teenager in his bedroom and has bec among the oldest independent publishing houses in Portl OR. We are a politically moderate, centrist publisher i world that has inched to the right for the past 80 years.

INTRODUCTION

It's April 2020. My small business has lost its primary income source. My best friend from childhood is dead from the novel coronavirus. And I don't know how to parent through this kind of grief.

With school canceled for the foreseeable future, I am all things to my two daughters: playmate and authority figure, teacher and counselor, news reporter and fairytale teller, complaint department and conflict resolution bureau. When I fall apart, when I let myself cry, when I can't help letting the grief and worry show through, they panic.

Being sad means I loved my friend, I tell them.

Sometimes crying is the best way to work through a hard thing.

It's not healthy to pretend we are okay when we are not okay.

Saying these things with tears rolling down my face doesn't reassure my daughters. It only makes them more desperate to distract me, console me, tickle me into smiling. My husband tries to draw them away so I can grieve in private, but my sadness ignites their anxiety and they won't leave me alone.

There is no such thing as private when sheltering in place Even locking myself in the bathroom doesn't work for long The girls can sense my emotion flooding through the house It's an unmistakable perfume, grief. They find me and knock until I relent and let them in. My tears drip down their swee foreheads and they suffer my hugs and sniffles.

When they can't take the wet mess of me any longer, they ask, *Are you better now?*

No, I say, *but let's go play cribbage.*

It's messy and chaotic, parenting through a crisis, but I have to hope on some level, it's a comfort for them. To see a hear break and stay broken while responsibilities push up through the wreckage like fresh grass.

They are bearing witness to how I, despite my grief, make i through the day.

GRASS

I cannot think about the future.

Instead I sit in the grass and listen to the few cars rolling by behind our house. This is a pause between duties, just one way to wait for a child to need me for something. Right now, though: the grass. It makes my ankles itchy. I'm allergic. I get hives and sneezes erupt. But it feels good, letting the earth hold me, so I stay put for a while longer.

It's not brave, doing nothing in the backyard, keeping away from the news. But it's how I am getting through. Soon enough one of the kids will find me to inquire or complain about something that doesn't really matter.

Who cares who goes first in the game when people are dying?

I don't know where you put your hairbrush.

Can't you fix it for her? Please?

Right now, though, it's quiet.

Just a few more minutes alone will help me make it through the next hour.

Please

scream

inside

your

heart

VOCABULARY

Tracy, my eight-year-old, mixed up *academic* and *epidemic* during our first week of virus-mandated homeschool. This slip delighted me.

Then we added *pandemic* and *social distance* to her internal dictionary. And now we are redefining the word *container*—how it refers to our immediate household, not just the school lunch we don't need to pack anymore.

There are four of us in our container in Portland, Oregon. I do not go anywhere, except in the yard or for occasional walks with a mask. How could I leave my house in these times and not betray my friend Priya? Her last words to me, via text, were these:

"I hope your family and extended family are all well and safe. Please keep your kids and family away from anyone else right now."

I can't imagine going out anytime soon, resuming any sort of *normal* that involves other people being within six feet of me. Even though I know Priya didn't expect me to put my life on hold forever, I have her words to steer me. Her concern carves strict boundaries between our container and the rest of the world.

So I stay home with Holly, age twelve, and Tracy. I act as their teacher and activity director while working on my business, meeting deadlines, taking calls, and sending emails. My husband comes back from his outings with groceries, toilet paper, and other provisions. I yearn for that kind of freedom, for that semblance of normalcy, but I'm too scared to go anywhere.

Priya didn't mean for me to stay away from people for the whole rest of my life. She just asked me to be careful.

I like to think I will go out again when it's safe.

My Grief Resumé

- My childhood dog.
- Two grandmas.
- Two grandpas.
- One great-grandpa.
- My father-in-law.

I am an only child. Both of my parents are still here. Not here, in person, but alive in their container, three thousand miles away from the future they are planning here in Portland, Oregon. This makes me incredibly privileged. But it also means I don't have enough experience with grief to be able to explain it to my children when my best friend gets sick, goes to the hospital, and dies.

Priya Khanna has been one of my best friends since fifth grade, when I was ten and she was almost ten. My daughters at eight and twelve now make the math work out to plus two and minus two. This feels, somehow, significant. A context that will help them understand the scope of our friendship. We *were just two years older than you when we met,* I tell Tracy. *Just two years younger than you*, I tell Holly.

Priya lived in the red house on the corner, ten houses and one left turn away from my house in New Jersey. We didn't know each other until I changed schools that year and met her. Priya played clarinet; I studied flute. We were woodwinds together. We wrote each other tiny notes in math class on the backs of Beech-Nut mint wrappers. We went trick-or-treating. She told me when I didn't understand social cues and messed up, and she gave me the space to apologize.

In the summers, our parents let us venture down the big hill and past the empty park to the closest tennis court. Priya had a muscular serve, a power I couldn't match. I darted and dove for balls and skinned my knees and lost games to her. If our parents gave us money, we went to pizza afterwards. Once, we interrupted a late-afternoon meeting of men in dark suits and sunglasses. They sat in the corner, their backs to the wall, shifting to glance at us. The restaurant was empty except for us two and our slices and the men. We ate quickly and left, bursting into the sunlight, whispering, *The mafia!* Giddy from being so close to possible danger and surviving.

Priya grew up to follow her older sister and parents into the medical profession. She helped her college and med school friends study for tests. She excelled as a nephrologist, her chosen specialty. She saved lives. But the hospital staff couldn't save her.

This is the last text I sent her, on the day intubation seemed imminent. You can see the hurry in my scissor marks:

you

BRAVE and

THE MEANING OF CLOSENESS

Our friendship with the next-door neighbors feels more like we are family. The mom grew up in a kibbutz and this shared, collective mentality is one we strive to emulate. Before the pandemic, our kids wandered in and out of each other's houses. We walked to school together. The children played all afternoon, every afternoon, and the parents fed whoever came into our kitchens.

When the stay-at-home statewide order took effect, we kept up our playtime—just with that one family—but then the governor established shelter-in-place, which came with different rules. No-contact ones. Six feet apart. We obeyed immediately and stayed inside, afraid our children wouldn't follow the new protocols and we might get each other sick.

We used to measure our closeness to the next-door neighbors by group dinners, being an audience for the kids' plays, evening bonfires, snow days, hand-me-down clothes exchanges, trading bikes, blackberry picking. Now, in discussing *how close we are* to our neighbors, we are addressing physical distance. We need more of it to stay healthy, but we want less of it. Our days are shaped by this push-pull. Creating boundaries around human want.

During those early weeks, whenever our kids wanted to go outside, an adult had to tag along to model appropriate behavior, offer social distancing reminders, and perform visible responsibility. If we let the kids outside without supervision, even though they have been playing outside safely for years, it might look to others on the street that we didn't care about the new rules. An adult presence, to the people walking by, meant it was safe to walk past our house.

As more information has come out about COVID-19, and we have grown more settled in this new eerie no-touch world, our kids have adjusted and adapted. My girls and the next-door neighbor kids now play in one yard or the other without touching, without forgetting themselves, without an adult standing guard over their relationships. They can be trusted to bike around the block without getting too close to each other. They can build imaginary worlds with words instead of props. They know to step back on the grass to avoid anyone walking on the sidewalk.

It's a huge relief to hear voices in the front yard when I do dishes. Not normal, because the children are not shoulder to shoulder or sharing craft supplies, but they are together.

Laughter floats through the tree branches. If I don't look out the window, it almost doesn't feel like a crisis.

There's an unexpected benefit to sheltering at home. I don't have to perform social greetings or meet expectations of what a forty-something-year-old should wear or do. As a neurodivergent person, this carries a sense of relief, a loosening of expectations. It's okay to feel too much right now.

This permission I am giving myself—under the auspices of quarantine—applies to the inside of the house as well. I don't pick up toys and books in the living room unless I want to, because it's just us. I don't care what my kids' rooms look like. They pull clean clothes out of a laundry basket. Pick mismatched socks or go barefoot.

Holly wrote a logic essay for school about why she shouldn't have to clean her room during a pandemic.

"Cleaning is a waste of time right now. I'd rather do an art project," she wrote.

These days, the girls and I can spend the whole day in pajamas if we want to, unless my husband says otherwise.

It's a social rule he likes: getting dressed for the day. He believes in routine as a way forward in uncertain times. This helps, because I cannot see past my grief. At least one of us has a plan. At least one of us can see a purpose in creating and meeting expectations.

I have to admit getting dressed seems to help my mood. On days I stay in pajamas, I am more likely to crawl back into bed and sob. Let the hurt in me blur the moment, turn everything into hazy blobs, only keeping my grief in focus. As much as I want the flexibility to cry alone, I am glad when my husband encourages me to face the day.

The Cousin Becky rule—wear shoes on bikes—still applies in this alternate reality, along with our insistence on helmets. I'm not even sure exactly what happened to Cousin Becky—a foot injury, certainly, maybe a hospital trip? It's my husband's story, a holdover from his childhood.

Cousin Becky rule! my kids shout to each other. Sometimes they race inside to tell us about a kid from down the street riding barefoot. Then we talk about how different parents set different expectations. The social distancing rule washes across everything, though. All neighborhood kids are expected to stand one bike length away or farther no matter what. The distance from one side of the garage door to the other is also a good measure. Anything closer is not allowed.

Distance! the kids have learned to shout at each other. *You're getting too close.*

ONLINE SCHOOL

The first few weeks of the pandemic, when it still felt like an adventure, Holly's charter school quickly pivoted to full-time online lessons, but Tracy went to Mommy School. We built in opera and baking, reading and biking. Garden class happened every Tuesday. Holly joined us for art, PE, and snack and story, then wandered back to her Chromebook to check in with her actual teachers.

A mandatory Mommy School unit on the Hero's Journey netted ongoing conversations about books and movies—*she's the gatekeeper! The protagonist is in the wasteland now.* We decided *we* are in the wasteland too and began looking for the helpers and the elixirs.

But then online school started for Tracy. She already knows all the grade-appropriate math concepts and how to dissect a story. She can write and read, tell time and count coins. Moving boxes around on a screen to show what she already knows feels fruitless. Boring. And it doesn't come with the social interaction that fueled her love of in-person school.

Holly's teachers, on the other hand, incorporate real-world concepts and learning. She is asked to identify three plants in the yard that she doesn't know. Math includes making a map of the back yard, figuring out the dimensions, and helping her teacher figure out how much paint he needs for a certain room. For humanities, she studies dystopian literature and thinks about our current altered reality through this lens.

Online school means a lot more screen time than we like. And our daughters have learned to click over to something more interesting when we *think* they are in school. There's grief here. And also resignation. We have to pass the hours. I have actual career work to do, deadlines to meet and emails to send. Sometimes I need the kids to be on their computers so I can get something done even if it means stepping across a pre-established boundary. We are, we remind each other, mid-crisis.

Tracy didn't even have a computer before this; a family friend gave her an old laptop when we realized what the future looked like. The machine is heavy and awkward on her lap, but it's hers. And all she wants—at a time in her life when she can't bounce next door into her best friend's house, or let him bounce into hers—is that screen. It's not really learning, not even when she's listening to the rules and clicking through her assignments. She gets more out of a walk in the woods with me, thinking about whether she gets wetter under the trees because of raindrops rolling off leaves or out in the open, in the middle of a deserted street, and whether the puddle she admired yesterday will be bigger or smaller today.

To establish more real-world moments, I have taken to hiding her computer and claiming it has gone out for sushi. Her computer gets terribly hungry. It is sad about all the time it spends alone in the house. It really wants avocado rolls. Sometimes the computer has a beer or a glass of wine after sushi and then to be a good citizen, it has to wait for a while, until it's safe to drive home.

When Tracy's computer goes out for sushi, we read. We make comics. We paint. We run circles in the yard, pretending to be kittens. It doesn't matter if she doesn't turn in all her assignments.

The pandemic's effect on time, the realization that the day of the week doesn't matter, is a reason to let go of more parenting and school expectations. We have tomorrow coming. And the day after that. We'd better take care of our emotional needs today. We'd better say *okay* to ourselves and let ourselves off the hook. We'll try again in the morning.

Emergency Worm

When I was a child, at bedtime, my dad told me invented-on-the-spot Murphy Stories, about a little boy who was very impy. At bedtime in our house, my husband tells the girls Riley and Regan ghost stories and Danny and Michelle hospital stories.

I studied *The Decameron* in college. Giovanni Boccaccio, writing in the fourteenth century, sends his characters away from the city so they can escape the plague. The ten young people in *The Decameron* keep themselves occupied in quarantine by telling a hundred stories. In some ways, this is our life now. There are lots of stories. Tracy's computer going out for sushi is one.

One night, at bedtime, Tracy wanted me to tell a Danny and Michelle story, which aren't my stories, but sometimes if she's anxious and my husband is busy, I relent and tell one.

Danny and Michelle are friends. They work at the hospital. Danny works as a chef in the commissary and Michelle is an emergency room nurse.

This one night, trying to goad me into imagining, Tracy started off the story and said *emergency room*, and I said, *emergency WORM?*

Room, she clarified.

Worm! I said.

R-O-O-M, she spelled.

We cracked ourselves up thinking about an emergency worm.

The next morning, Tracy decided she wanted to write a chapter book about Emergency Worm. This became part of

Mommy School. She spoke the adventures to me and I typed them.

Emergency Worm lives in a flower pot next to the hospital gift shop. She helps patients feel better. She travels around the hospital by zipline. In the second chapter, a fungus covers the city. It's not safe to touch anything.

"Everyone is trapped in their car or their house because of the fungus," Tracy dictated. "The fungus was white and gooey. It was really gross. And it was really poisonous. If you touched it or ate it, you would get sick, and you would have to go to the hospital. But if you don't get immediate care, something bad happens. We can't tell you what will happen."

Being sick from the fungus means going to the hospital.

If you don't get care, something bad will happen.

We can't tell you what.

I
WISH
THIS
WERE
A
PANDA-EMIC.

THE OTHER HOUSE

Unlike most families, there is one place we can go without fear of cross-contamination. My parents' new house is six minutes away from ours. They are sheltering-in-place on the East Coast, so we can use their house as a second container, as if we are salad being transferred from one bowl to another.

Same quarantine, different furniture.

Now we call Grandma and Grandpa's new house *the other house* or we don't call it anything at all. If I say, *Let's go,* the destination is implied. There's nowhere else I am comfortable going.

At the other house, the top of the dishwasher doesn't hold when it's loaded; one side loses its grip and falls lower than the normal side. The ants are still an issue. But the yard! I am here for each sprout, each new bud. Tiny oak trees grow from forgotten acorns by the side of the house; they need to be pinched out by my girls and me, one at a time so we get the roots. Sometimes the whole acorn comes up and we can study how new life has cracked forth. How stubborn and optimistic the roots are.

My parents are missing spring here in Oregon. They cannot smell their lilacs, arrange bouquets of their dazzling tulips, or marvel at the bright orange azaleas that rise like a flame in the middle of the back yard. They are not here for birdsong. To cut the grass. Or to watch petals drift off the dogwoods—pale pink and white—like a setting for a wedding. They cannot rub the wandering mint between their thumb and forefinger or admire the sudden abundance of new growth on the trellis. Behold: grapes!

I send my parents pictures. Of the cut flowers. The rhododendrons. The hostas. Each new discovery of spring—what shade of green is this?

On rainy days, when we are at their house, we FaceTime them from our "islands" in the empty living room: another game we've invented. Tracy takes the rectangle of memory foam as her territory. Holly pushes two soft pillows together and kneels so her sister can't steal them. I am left with a used paper envelope as my shelter. It's the perfect metaphor for parenting: they are well provisioned and comfortable and I am left with what nobody else wants.

We "row" between the islands in our "boat"—a person-sized blue bag—using our palms to scoot our bodies forward.

Tracy maneuvers the boat by standing and jumping. This makes her the fastest of us. Holly and I acknowledge there is nowhere else to go. Getting there slower means another few seconds we can fill with this game.

My parents cannot visit our islands or sit on the back porch. They are not here to make coffee their way. To fight the ants. To troubleshoot the upstairs toilet. To remind Tracy not to splash in the bathtub. There are new weeds to pinch out every time we visit. These are our jobs now.

It feels good to have something to do.

GRIEFING

Losing your ability to attend school can cause grief. Not being able to go to the park or see friends: more grief. Holly laments the canceled trip to Seattle, an early virus hotbed. She misses her friends and teachers. She wishes for the contents of her locker. She can't even walk to the ice cream parlor with a neighbor anymore. Or walk anywhere without a mask.

Early on in the pandemic, I worried about my business, a small publishing house, and grieved the closing of independent bookstores, my main customers. But then Priya and her family got sick and a bigger, deeper grief subsumed me.

On April 13, the day Priya died, I stayed in bed all morning. Couldn't get up. The kids came and went with kisses and notes. Tracy suggested that Priya could be my imaginary friend now, so I could have her with me always. I laughed-cried and told her this was a very good idea.

My friend Liz offered to come over and break the social distancing rule to give me a hug. I wanted that hug so much, but I feared it'd break me. That a hug, once given, meant starting from scratch getting used to the absence of them. That it'd be harder, in the future, to keep my distance. Priya had said stay inside, stay safe, and I wanted to keep Liz safe too. So I declined and thanked her.

By the afternoon, Holly wouldn't get out of bed. She assessed my coping mechanism and decided to adapt it for herself. After all, she could play games on her computer or listen to her favorite songs. Being in bed meant not having to deal with the rest of the family. It meant darkness and blankets.

She didn't get out of bed the next day, even though I got up to model some semblance of normal. She didn't get out of bed the day after that, either. She wanted to stay in her room. Away from the unpredictability of her mother's waves of sadness.

Holly wrote to her teacher: "I feel so alone because I have no one my age to hang out with and my mom is in deep grief cause of her friend dying and my sister not being herself cause the grief rubbed off on me and my sister so I have been hiding from everyone because I don't no how to deal with my mom when she is griefing."

I reached out to Holly's school counselor, who invited us to an online session. Holly wanted me to join and I agreed as long as we took the call anywhere but her bed. We set up my laptop in the downstairs office, squeezed together in a rolling chair. The counselor asked questions and listened and gave us homework: self-care. I suggested we make lists and Holly could watercolor the backgrounds the way she did for our homeschool rules list, which hangs on the garage door as a reminder that this is an eating space, a living space, and also a learning space.

That afternoon, Holly and I brainstormed ways we could make ourselves feel better. I didn't dare acknowledge, *You are out of bed!* Or she might crawl back in.

Our lists have a lot of the same things on them:

- Knitting
- Games
- Art
- Books
- Exercise

Holly asked me to write her list for her, spacing each word floating far enough from the others so she can put blue tape over them before painting watercolors over the top. Each word will have white space around it. The paint will fill in the rest of the paper with soft, evocative color.

When she saw my list, Tracy grabbed a pen and added, "Forging about Priy."

She meant forgetting. If I can just forget about my friend, I won't be sad anymore. That's what Tracy thinks.

Oh sweetie, I said to her. *That's not how it works. I'm sad because I loved her so much.*

Holly added paint, making my list into sherbet hues: red, orange, yellow.

Tracy's wish for me to forget about Priya touches *bath, word games, writing,* and *exercise.* I don't know how to explain the sweetness in remembering. How essential it is to love like that. How I am the person I am because Priya loved me.

But we aren't going anywhere, we don't have plans except for the online lessons their teachers organize, so I will find a way to explain, to model what it means to love and lose.

We will learn about grief together. It's the only way forward. As much as I'd like everything to be fine, I don't have the energy to pretend. I miss Priya too much.

FUN:

PRE-EMPTED

BY

THE

PANDEMIC

GIFT

In lieu of a hug, my friend Liz dropped off a beautiful present.

With art supplies she found around her house, she created a representation of Priya's sparkly pink cell phone case, seen in a recent photo shared online. The amount of time and care and glue that went into that gift made me feel so grateful for Liz's friendship.

I couldn't reach out and hug Priya or her family, so Liz brought me a talisman. Something to hold. I sobbed and laughed when she left it on my doorstep. Priya would have loved its colors, its bright elegance, how much thought had gone into recreating the phone case she loved.

It's perfect, I told Liz.

I keep the gift displayed on my dresser, and I turn it from side to side. Priya's face some days. The pink glam side on others.

ONE PROJECT A DAY

Priya's father died eight days after she did. He was also a doctor, also stricken by the virus.

"Grief changes as we go through it," I wrote in my quarantine journal the afternoon of her father's funeral service. "Today was hard. I have never grieved like this. Like a throat has opened up and then closed around me. I couldn't help my kids today. I couldn't do anything."

I am still there, in the throat.

Sometimes, I think to myself, *I am so sad I want to die*, and yet I don't actually mean it. I am just so tired and so sad. That's what I say when people ask: *I am still so sad*. Those days, the ones when I want everything to go away, the pressure to ease, I pick an art project to work on or I go back to bed for a nap.

Projects, I have come to realize, help more than sleep. After a nap, I rise to the same reality, but if I can paint or draw or bake or pull an hour's worth of weeds, my day changes in a small but measurable way.

Each piece of work feels close to joy, or at least as close as I can get within the fog of grief. I always thought you had to make something perfect to be proud of it, but mid-crisis, I am letting that go. It doesn't have to be great art or cake for me to feel better during and after the making.

While virtually attending Priya's prayer service, I decided projects could be my way forward. I would create something with my hands every day. Just one thing. It could be more, it could be many things per day, but I would focus on one. The journal I choose to track my daily projects is flecked with tiny wild strawberries. A gift from a former classmate. The marbled bookplate first page says "To Laura from Laura, 12/25/92."

Priya knew Laura. I think she would have liked me using this high school present as a way to move forward now. I haven't stayed in touch with Laura, but Priya's death has gotten our class of 1994 to reach out to each other through social media, texting, phone calls, and even a class Zoom. It's good to see everyone. I cry in front of my classmates, even the popular ones, and I do not say much, but we are all together while still in our containers.

Day by day, the evidence of getting through another day collects around me. Cards in envelopes, waiting to be mailed. A batch of peanut butter brownies. A sweater made of sock yarn scraps growing from my needles.

My sourdough starter behaves. I talk to it and encourage it to feed and make my bread rise. My sourdough starter doesn't hold grudges about yesterday or yell like my kids do when they get annoyed with each other. It doesn't dare cheat at games. It doesn't argue, *I don't want to do that right now!* Homemade sourdough crackers replace all salty snacks because they are a renewable resource, easy to replace as long as we have flour. I snack on crackers the way I used to reach for chocolate.

I thank my husband every time he brings home another precious bag of flour. I keep my knitting by my chair. I wash paint brushes in the laundry room sink and take an online art class to learn new techniques.

Our friend Edith always brings us paper bags filled with odds and ends, sometimes whole stacks of matching scrapbook paper. I can make as many cards as I want and still have supplies for more. I address envelopes for the finished ones in batches, then ask Holly to walk with me to the postal box up the hill near our house. We wear our matching purple masks. I bring a tissue to use to hold the blue handle of the mail drop box.

By ask, I mean insist. Every time we take this journey—our own micro adventure into the wasteland and back—Holly complains about how far it is midway up the big hill. At that point, we still have to get to the box, turn around, and go home. She begs to stand there on the sidewalk waiting for me instead of coming all the way.

She used to take walking field trips with her school. She used to spend Tuesdays at a watershed, often in the rain, identifying plants and taking water quality samples. Now leaving our block feels too far. Even with masks. The wasteland metaphor, perhaps, is something she feels in her muscles and joints. She wants to go home.

Sometimes on the journey, usually between complaints, Holly reaches for my hand. Here we are, on the verge of her being a teenager, and she wants that connection. Our walks are special, and she feels it, even if I have to make them mandatory for her to participate.

We are out together, in the wide world, and a few days from now, our friends will open their mailboxes and find a bit of cheer inside.

ART

IS

MY

MAP

Both at Once

"Love not grief," Tracy tells me.

She is young enough still to expect one or the other. She wants the happy one to replace the sad one.

But they are held together in my heart: *love* and *grief*.

Barefoot

I don't wear shoes in quarantine. With unmatched socks and warm-enough weather, it makes sense to go barefoot. Who cares if I am not acting like all the other adults on the block? One day, though, I scratch a deep gouge into the top of my left foot when I get too close to the bed frame.

The cut is slow to scab. I cannot put on shoes comfortably, even if I want to. I keep it open to the air during the day and bandage it at night. I cannot go to the other house because I cannot drive without shoes because that is a rule I have always kept, even during a crisis. Then Holly finds my blue sparkly Mary Janes in the closet.

Try these, she urges. *Just try them.*

And sure enough, the shoes arc around the cut as if they are made for this purpose: the strap below, the toe above. I can walk in these. I can garden in these. I can drive to the other house in these.

Once, a million story-years ago like everything from *before*, I wore these shoes when a pit bull leapt over its fence and attacked me and the girls on our walk to school. I hiked Tracy up my side, held her on my shoulder, and shoved Holly behind me. I kicked into the pit bull's mouth with one blue sparkly Mary Jane. I screamed for help, many times, and nobody heard. Not one neighbor came outside in our close-knit community.

I got tired but kept kicking. Afraid I'd lose my balance and drop Tracy. The dog kept barking and baring its teeth, a bite imminent. I kicked until I couldn't hold on any longer, my left leg still holding me up and me holding Tracy up, acting as a human shield, best I could, for Holly. Knowing soon I would fall. Knowing I couldn't keep this up.

I have always loved dogs, and I felt insane and horrible kicking one, defending my children from these jaws and not actually having the situation change one bit. My standing leg got more and more tired. I didn't want to fall or drop Tracy.

So I did the thing you're not supposed to do. I pushed Holly ahead of me and we ran away, Tracy still clinging to me, into the open garage of a neighbor. Then I squished both girls between the storm door and the wooden house door, banging and screaming for help before turning to face the dog myself.

I knew I would get bitten and that was better than my children getting bitten. I blocked them both in that door triangle, hoped desperately that the neighbor was home and hadn't just forgotten to close his garage door before going to work.

Then, a surprise, one that saved us. That dog stopped on the threshold, still barking and showing its teeth, but not daring to cross the scent barrier.

You walk down a street every weekday for years, and it's always safe. You don't worry about the dog until the dog finds you. And then you can't walk down the street without thinking about the dog.

This, somehow, feels like a microcosm of parenting during a pandemic. You have to make decisions from a place of fear and exhaustion and what information you have in the moment. Without knowing what's next. Without knowing what's right.

Role Reversal

Me, checking my email: *Oh, another rejection.*

Holly: *Who cares? You're amazing. You're a great writer.*

I have talked to her for years about grades and mistakes and rejections, but always as her cheerleader and her champion. Now, in these circumstances, she has figured out how to be mine.

I Said a Terrible Thing

One afternoon, when Tracy saw grief blooming on my face, she pressed a moldy cherry tomato against my lips, trying to get me to eat it. As a joke. To make me laugh so I wouldn't cry.

I clenched my lips and teeth closed just in time. The juices ran out and dripped on my shirt. Then I burst into tears and screamed, *How could you do this to me?*

Her face, suddenly stricken. She hadn't expected this big of a reaction. She had wanted to be funny.

Here, the container failed. Broke apart. For all our best intentions, emotional exhaustion leads to a collapse. To a mother saying to a surprised child, *How could you do this to me?*

I didn't care about the spots on my shirt, but her glee felt so personal and I am allergic to mold. She cried, and I did too, and we hugged, and then we began again.

A GOOD DAY

We go to my parents' house and there's sun! And it's hot!

I put the seedlings on the front walkway to drowse in the sun, and get stronger, and we wander to different parts of the yard and house. We enjoy having space from each other for a while.

I forgot the starts, though, and they bent and wilted. The carrots mostly, and some of the cucumbers. I planted a few in the garden beds, anyway, hoping life might surge forth, but not expecting it.

We should plant more seeds. Try again. I apologize to the girls for my inattention. They apologize for theirs, because they could have rescued the plants or reminded me to check on them.

I think I was sun-drunk that day, wandering around barefoot on the back patio, eyeing lilacs and the curling green of grapevines emerging from the brittle wooden husks now that winter is gone, while they danced and listened to music and flipped on the TV, because we don't have TV at home.

A lightness in my heart.

The grief was still there, deep and urgent, but I could hear the birds, feel the wind. My hands-on project for the day was planting those struggling seedlings. Plunging my fingers into the dirt. Thinking of the future.

The starts didn't survive. We haven't yet planted new seeds. But it's okay. Not all the time, but sometimes, I can hold that lightness in my heart even when it's raining. Just a few weeks ago, I couldn't feel anything good at all.

GAME NIGHT

We play Yahtzee over the phone with Auntie Donna.

Holly holds her ears when her sister shakes the dice in the cup. Tracy shakes and shakes and shakes, with the persistence it takes to churn butter. The adults grin and wait.

We figure out a system with the phone—who gets to hold Auntie Donna when. So it's fair. When Auntie Donna rolls, we set the phone flat in the center of the kitchen table and lean our faces in close. She sees chin, eyeball, hair. We wait and wonder and listen.

Auntie Donna wins, because she's the only one with a Yahtzee. The rest of us take zeros there. Auntie Donna's luck is with aces. The smallest, least consequential number. Five ones win her the game.

We plan to play every Sunday and then the next Sunday comes and we don't call each other, but another quarantine Sunday is coming. We can do it next time. There is no overlay of guilt, no regret. No need to forgive ourselves for missing.

RAIN

Holly eyes the rain from the doorway, grins, then runs outside, arms wide in welcome. I laugh and follow her, barefoot. We mark the wet grass with prints. How come she has her shoes on? I know why I don't: today is not a shoe day. Hers are thick, black, waterproof. Shoes meant for December, for the environmental study project her class worked on all last term. She doesn't have shoes for May because we have not gone into the world in search of them.

She races up the steep incline of Rosemary's driveway and waits for me. I catch up, in a slow-motion hobble, saying *Ow!* because my heels are cracked from going barefoot on hot pavement.

Ready? she asks.

I can't race, I tell her.

It's not a race, she clarifies. *Just run with me. It's okay.*

I run with her.

It's okay.

CLOTHING

Why not wear something I love every day?

Why am I saving it all for *later*?

Out with the button downs! Out with the scratchy seams!

Bring on the soft black leggings with gold unicorns, the embroidered tunic, the *Heartfirst* shirt designed by my friend Jess.

I wear a T-shirt over leggings into the yard one morning, and a curious girl from across the street asks, "Are those your pajamas?"

"No," I tell her, grinning. Then I wander back inside. I had forgotten to put on a skirt. But who cares? It's my yard. It's my quarantine. I kind of love that I confused her.

GLASS

I am doing better but I am still crying a lot.

I get on Zoom calls with friends and my eyes fill because they are not Priya, or because someone inevitably asks, *How are you doing?* And I have never been able to lie.

My friend Kathleen emails after one of these: "I see so much sadness in your eyes when we're on Zoom. I am thinking of you and here for you if you need an ear."

Everyone can see my grief, even through the screen.

One morning, when I carried a glass of water into the living room, Tracy asked:

"Let me just ask a question. Is that water or tears?"

"Um. Water?"

She said, "With you, it's more likely to be tears."

I am moving forward, being present, but I am not the same as before.

Here sits Laura, on the couch, with her glass full of tears.

COMPLETION

My projects inspire Holly to sew, knit, bake, and make art—all things on her self-care list. One night, she spends hours punching *V* shapes out of a piece of decorative paper and gluing them onto a wooden bird form, like feathers.

She's not doing it just to complete the task, like usual. She is thinking about each piece of paper. *Does it go here?* Or *here?* She works hard and goes to bed long after me.

When I wake, I am devastated to see she has finished both sides of the bird. I wanted her to have something to look forward to when she woke up.

But she wanted to be done. To wake up finished and pleased with the result.

The distance between what I want and what she wants sometimes gets filled with loudness, with sadness, with uncertainty.

But then I remember, *These are both appropriate ways to be.*

The Next Apocalypse

It's bedtime in the new normal, which starts at 7 and stretches to 10 or 11, depending on how much reading is needed for Tracy to feel safe. The anxiety gets worse at night.

So when she asks, "When's the next apocalypse?" I understand. She wants to know. Have some more warning next time.

Everything has changed, and for a kid who likes everything the same, a transition would have made it smoother.

She is staring at the full moon, though, and I realize she means *eclipse.*

Hawk

Tracy begs me to close my eyes. She leads me to emerald grass, under the giant oak tree, and then tells me to open them.

This is where we'll read. She helps herself to my lap, making a pillow of my feet, stretching out like my legs are her bed. It's not particularly comfortable for either of us, but we have this tree, these birds, this book.

She spots a hawk, circling, and worries aloud that it might be circling us. Her anxiety levels have skyrocketed since Priya's death. She asks about death and wants to know if everyone dies and she marks threats like this hawk. She wants to know if we could be prey to a bird that knows how to fly like that.

I point out the two little birds, singing angry songs, diving at the hawk, trying to chase it away. And they do. Then we look back at the book, *The Great Upending* by Beth Kephart, and I raise my eyebrows and point at the cover.

She sits up and squeals. "Hawk!"

It's the name of the protagonist's brother.

A few days later, under the giant oak, we find fluffy baby bird feathers, tufts of gray and white, and a bloody red claw, left behind.

"Hawk," we say to each other.

I can hear

the wind

here

OBITUARY

From a feature story in *The Guardian*, I learned the details of Priya's time in the hospital. How the crisis impacted available supplies. How she kept in touch with a physician covering her patients from her hospital bed.

The article came out on May 20, a month and a week after her death. I know two friends of the reporter's and helped her connect to the family. A quote of mine is in there. The world knows, now, about Priya and her dad. The grief that family carries. How they served their patients. And how much Priya was loved. It's a tribute, a lovely tribute, and it's also incredibly traumatic to read these details. To know this much more.

I couldn't handle my sadness so I let my kids start the day with online games and then ordered macarons from a local bakery I like to support. In a few hours, sugar would be coming to our doorstep, no-contact delivery, and I am the worst human in the whole world because I clicked pay before adding a tip of 20 percent, which I have done on all the other orders. I am so dumb. I am so angry at myself.

Then I realize this wave is because I talked to the reporter and couldn't control the outcome. And I urged the sisters to talk to the reporter. How the article is so good and so sad. How they used my photos and credited the Khanna family, and how that feels right, being credited as part of the family, but the sisters didn't share any.

I didn't know a patient coughed right in Priya's face. Then she got sick.

I didn't know how she got to the ambulance or what our friend Justin said to her when the paramedics took her away.

I knew she wanted a blanket and couldn't get one, but I didn't know they weren't feeding her or monitoring her the whole time.

A macaron shaped like a banana isn't going to change the knowing I wish I didn't have. I wrote an email to the bakery asking to contact me so I can add a tip. This helps, a little, but not as much as telling my kids how I feel.

"I need your help today," I said. "An article came out. I'm really sad. I need you to do something with me."

Holly and Tracy came up with a plan: we will dye the tips of our hair with sugar-free raspberry Jell-O. Holly sets up the salon and goes first. Thirty minutes of dunking. I help her wrap a sopping towel around the dripping red mass of her ponytail, and when she returns from the shower, I cannot tell that the color has changed, but she says it has, so then it's Tracy's turn. Then mine. I change into pajamas and settle in, head tilted back. By now, the water has cooled. The red liquid is solidifying. Thirty minutes later, when I pull my ponytail out, it is covered in clumps of artificially flavored gelatin.

A few years back, Priya met me in New York and treated me to high tea at The Plaza. I selected the Eloise tea for kids instead of something more sophisticated, more in keeping with the fancy location and with me being an adult. Priya was delighted because I was delighted. The Eloise tea came with cotton candy. We marveled over each luxurious bite, each sip, and being together in the city. Just like when we were in high school and used to bus our way in.

I can't tell that anything has changed from dipping my hair into Jell-O, but I do feel better. Despite a stiff neck. The macarons arrive. They help too. I eat a pink-and-blue one, cotton-candy flavor, and recall tea at The Plaza.

MEMORIES

The girls fight a lot. It's like a pressure cooker, this container. On one occasion, Holly retreats to her bedroom and Tracy pushes pictures of her sister under the door, taken with a Polaroid camera. They are from happier times.

Tracy says, *When I get a feeling in the pit of my stomach from fighting with Sissy, I want her to remember what it was like before.*

When you loved each other? I ask, feeling overwhelmed and frustrated and knowing I shouldn't ask, but the words slip out anyway.

Tracy nods. She sees me understanding what she means, even if I shouldn't have said it like that. That's why she has sent these pictures by door-mail.

I am too sad to explain that they still love each other, that this anger is a product of crisis, of being cooped up together, of being home day after day after day. But even without my verbal processing, without prompting her to think about love and how tomorrow is another day, there's hope here. A fight and a reconciliation. A calling in, from one sister to the other.

Remember how things used to be?

Black Lives Matter

Police kill George Floyd on May 25, then protests erupt around the nation. We—white people who mean well—too often fall back on praising ourselves for being progressive, for listening to our friends of color, for reading deeply, and yet not much has changed.

We have to listen better.

We have to have these conversations with our kids.

We have to do better.

Together, as a family, all four of us talk about race and white privilege. We read books. We share racist incidents that have happened to our Black friends and explain the term *microaggressions*.

Tracy writes Black Lives Matter on a sign in her virtual house in her favorite game and she calls me over to show me. Anyone who visits her house will see this message. We talk about why All Lives Matter is offensive. When Tracy sees someone in the virtual schoolhouse has written this repellent version on the chalkboard, she gets upset and erases it. *Black Lives Matter*, she types, then reports this improvement to me.

Holly has learned about racism and what it means to be an anti-racist in school and at home. Her sixth-grade curriculum included studying the Black history of Portland. For a few days, Portland has a curfew related to the protests, and we talk about what it means to break a rule to make a point. Why it's important to do everything we can to insist on systemic change.

I want to drop, face-down on the Burnside Bridge with my hands behind my back with the protesters, but I am still carrying Priya's words in my heart.

I am scared to leave the house.

This is what my Black friends feel on an everyday basis.

This is why I should be out on the street tonight.

ANOTHER LOSS

This one I have held in my cupped hands for months, holding onto each moment, knowing time would run out. I've always known someday one of my authors would die.

Terminal cancer, Ramiza Shamoun Koya had told me in 2018 over tea, after I had made an offer for her debut novel. She let me know so I could change my mind if I wanted. Her trusting me with this personal situation made me even more certain. I loved her book and wanted to be her publisher. I promised if her health timeline changed, I'd do everything possible to make sure she saw her book into the world.

We became dear friends in the following months. We told our stories to each other over tea. We made elaborate plans for publicity, her book tour, all of it guided by her wishes and dreams, all of it informed by her health, knowing things might change. In December, her prognosis sharpened: six months at most. Which meant June. Her novel, *The Royal Abduls,* was due out on May 12.

My team went to work proofing the manuscript and getting the project to press between Christmas and the beginning of 2020. We reimagined the launch to be early and local. Over the next weeks and months, authors, booksellers, reviewers, journalists, bloggers, and our distributor all pitched in to give Ramiza a modified book launch experience. In February, she called me her perfectionist, and I thrilled at the pronoun. Not just anyone's perfectionist: hers.

And she told me I had done more than enough. That I should put my attention elsewhere now. She wrote:

> I love everything that you've done for me, I'm humbled and honored and—frankly—pretty stunned. Working with you is a dream come true.
>
> But, if I may, it's time to slow down. We have plenty to work with. You've accomplished miracles.

It didn't feel like miracles, especially when the pandemic started shutting down our city. Ramiza called me a few days before her Powell's launch, slated for March 15, and said, *I don't want anyone to risk their health for me.* I agreed and contacted the store as soon as we got off the phone. Ramiza put the health of her community first. A few hours later,

Powell's announced the cancellation of all events, and soon thereafter all three stores closed for the foreseeable future.

I am glad Ramiza had the agency to say *stop.* Not just about the event, but to me, her perfectionist.

In our last phone call, she told me how the pandemic shifted us all into her world, one where future plans cannot be made with certainty. She died June 5 at home, mid-pandemic, about three weeks after her official book launch.

The Royal Abduls cover depicts one light on in the evening in an upstairs window in Washington, DC. On our last tea date, Ramiza mentioned how she had been waking in the middle of the night to work on end-of-life to-do lists. In a house full of caretakers, she found her thinking and writing time while everyone else slept.

I told her, once she was gone, I would look at that cover and know it's her window, lighting the way.

Bedtime Conversation

Me: I miss my friends.

Tracy: I miss my friends too, Mama. I haven't seen Zoey since—

Me: But mine are dead.

Tracy: I see your point.

The next morning . . .

Tracy: Not all your friends are dead, Mama.

Early Morning

Walk past my house, and you might see me, pajama-clad and barefoot, swinging in the front yard hammock chair.

While my kids sleep late and my husband reads the news, I spin with the breeze and listen to birdsong. I use a small clay platter one of my daughters shaped and glazed as a place to dock my coffee between sips. The moss growing around the base of the tree tickles my toes when I unfold my legs. If I am not in the mood to be seen, I can gather the parachute fabric around my face when I hear footsteps on the sidewalk.

Here, in the hammock, I am most gentle with myself.

Parenting during a crisis has put me back into my body. Instead of making to-do lists and considering my next steps toward a deadline, I sway in the breeze, my feet getting cold, my stomach rumbling. In a minute, or maybe ten, I'll move toward a task, but right now, I am where I'm supposed to be. At home with my family, suspended between grief and hope. This is a sad house right now, but it's also full of art and laughter and hard conversations. All of us, like the plants in the garden, doing our best to grow.

PESTS UNITE!
MICROCOSM PUBLISHING.COM